THE ATLANTIC DIVISION

BY JIM GIGLIOTTI AND ROBERT E. SCHNAKENBERG

THE BOSTON CELTICS · THE NEW JERSEY NETS · THE NEW YORK KNICKS · THE PHILADELPHIA 76ERS · THE TORONTO RAPTORS

Published in the United States of America by
The Child's World® • PO Box 326
Chanhassen, MN 55317-0326

800-599-READ • www.childsworld.com

ACKNOWLEDGEMENTS

The Child's World®: Mary Berendes, Publishing Director

Editorial Directions, Inc.: E. Russell Primm, Editorial Director and Line Editor; Katie Marsico, Managing Editor; Caroline Wood, Editorial Assistant; Susan Hindman, Copy Editor; John Barrett, Proofreader; Tim Griffin, Indexer; Kevin Cunningham, Fact Checker; James Buckley Jr. and Jim Gigliotti, Photo Reseachers and Photo Selectors

Manuscript consulting and photo research by Shoreline Publishing Group LLC.

The Design Lab: Kathleen Petelinsek, Design and Page Production

Photos:
AP: 15
Andrew D. Bernstein/NBAE/Getty: 10
Bettmann/Corbis: 5, 7, 9, 23, 29, 30
Nathaniel S. Butler/NBAE/Getty: 19
Matt Campbell/AFP/Getty: 16
Darron Cummings/AP: 40
Jim Cummins/NBAE/Getty: 33
Moe Doiron/AP/CP: 36
Mark Duncan/AP: 1, 26
Frank Gunn/AP: 37
Walter Iooss, Jr./NBAE/Getty: 22, 32
Bill Kostroun/AP: Cover, 18, 20
Charles Krupa/AP: 12
Jim McKnight/AP: 13
Fernando Medina/NBAE/Getty: 41
NBAP/NBAE/Getty: 24
Doug Pensinger/Getty: 38
Reuters/Corbis: 35
Nick Wass/AP: 2
George Widman/AP: 34

**LIBRARY OF CONGRESS
CATALOGING-IN-PUBLICATION DATA**

Gigliotti, Jim.
   The Atlantic Division / by Jim Gigliotti and Robert Schnakenberg.
       p. cm. — (Above the rim)
   Includes index.
   ISBN 1-59296-525-3 (library bound : alk. paper)
   1. National Basketball Association—History—Juvenile literature. 2. Basketball—East (U.S.)—History—Juvenile literature. I. Schnakenberg, Robert. II. Title. III. Series
   GV885.515.N37G543   2006
   2005026207

TABLE OF CONTENTS

INTRODUCTION

Every sport has one legendary team. In baseball's major leagues, it's the New York Yankees. In the National Football League, it's the Green Bay Packers. In the National Hockey League, it's the Montreal Canadiens. They are the **flagship** franchises for each league, the ones that hang the most championship banners and the ones with the most historically interesting tradition and widespread following. In the National Basketball Association (NBA), that club is the Boston Celtics (sorry, Lakers fans).

By the end of the 2004–05 season, the Celtics had won a record 16 NBA titles, 23 division titles (and tied for two more), and 2,737 games. But it's not just the numbers. It's coach Red Auerbach and his victory cigar . . . Bob Cousy's behind-the-back passes . . . Bill Russell's rebounding and shot-blocking . . . John Havlicek's steals . . . Larry Bird's jumpers . . . even the grinning leprechaun mascot. They're all a big part of the NBA story.

The Celtics' presence alone would make the NBA's Atlantic Division steeped in history, because the team has been around for more than 50 years. But the division's tradition doesn't begin and end in Boston. Two other Atlantic Division franchises, the New York Knicks and the Philadelphia 76ers (originally the Syracuse Nationals), have been around since the beginning of the NBA. They were all playing when the new National Basketball Association

Hall of Fame point guard Bob Cousy helped build the Celtics' winning tradition.

was created following the unification of the Basketball Association of America (BAA) and the National Basketball League (NBL) in 1949–1950.

For two decades, those teams played in the NBA's Eastern Division. In 1970–71, the league expanded to 17 teams, and the Atlantic Division was born. The historic trio was joined that year by the expansion Buffalo Braves.

Since then, the division has undergone a few changes. When the New Jersey Nets entered the NBA in 1976–77 (they were still called the New York Nets at the time), they joined the Atlantic Division. Two years later, Buffalo moved to San Diego to become the Clippers (they're now in Los Angeles and the Pacific Division) and the Washington Bullets moved from the Central Division to the more geographically appropriate Atlantic. The Charlotte Hornets played their expansion year in the Atlantic and their second year in the Midwest Division, before moving to the Central in their third year. Expansion teams Miami and Orlando each played one season in the Western Conference before settling in the Atlantic. From the 1991–92 season through 2003–04, the division remained unchanged. Then in 2004–05, when the NBA realigned into six divisions, the Toronto Raptors joined the Celtics, Nets, Knicks, and 76ers to form a five-team Atlantic Division.

While Boston has the NBA's most storied tradition, the Celtics don't have exclusive rights to NBA lore. Read on, and you'll learn the rich traditions of the other established franchises in the Atlantic Division—and how the young franchise in Toronto is building its own history.

Team	Year Founded	Home Arena	Year Arena Opened	Team Colors
Boston Celtics	1946	**Fleet Center**	1995	**Green and white**
New Jersey Nets	1967	**Continental Airlines Arena**	1981	**Red, white, blue, gray, and silver**
New York Knicks	1946	Madison Square Garden	1968	Orange, white, and blue
Philadelphia 76ers	1949	Wachovia Center	1996	Black, gold, bronze, red, white, and blue
Toronto Raptors	1995	Air Canada Centre	1999	Red, purple, black, and silver

CHAPTER ONE

THE BOSTON CELTICS

Celtics coach Red Auerbach lit up a "victory cigar" after important wins.

The Celtics were founded as charter members of the BAA in 1946. Their first coach was John "Honey" Russell, and they made the **playoffs** in only their second season, in 1947–48. But to Boston fans, the real history of the Celtics began in 1950. That was the year the club laid the groundwork that made it the most dominant franchise in basketball history.

In 1950, the Celtics hired Red Auerbach as coach. Auerbach quickly found a center in Ed Macauley, who had played for the **defunct** St. Louis Bombers the previous year. Then, the Celtics got a little lucky. After the Chicago Stags folded, Boston, New York, and Philadelphia drew names of the Stags' three guards out of a hat. The Celtics drew rookie Bob Cousy. At the time, he was the least-desirable choice of the three. Eventually, Cousy made it into the Hall of Fame.

After finishing in last place in the Eastern Division in 1949–50, the Celtics made the playoffs in 1950–51. Auerbach continued to add pieces to the championship puzzle, including shooting guard Bill Sharman in 1951–52 and Frank Ramsey, the NBA's first true **sixth man,** in 1954–55. Boston won its first postseason series in 1952–53 and reached the playoffs each season through 1955–56, but bowed out every year before the finals.

The big breakthrough came in 1956–57. First, the Celtics selected Holy Cross's Tom Heinsohn in the draft. The team then traded Macauley and rookie Cliff Hagen to St. Louis in exchange for center Bill Russell.

After signing Heinsohn and Russell, everything fell into place. Heinsohn was a solid forward and the NBA's Rookie of the Year in 1956–57. Russell was a dominant defensive player and rebounder who went on to win five NBA Most Valuable Player (MVP) awards. Over the next 13 seasons, the Celtics ruled the NBA like no other team before or since.

Bill Russell was a dominant force on both offense and defense.

Boston won its first championship in 1956–57 with a thrilling 125–123 victory over the St. Louis Hawks in double overtime in Game 7 of the **NBA Finals.** St. Louis avenged that defeat in 1958, but the Celtics bounced back in 1958–59 to win the first of an unprecedented eight consecutive championships.

Over the years, the names of the players changed, but the Celtics maintained a legacy of success. Cousy retired after the club's fifth consecu-

The Celtics played their home games at Boston Garden from the inception of the franchise in 1946–47 through the 1994–95 season. They moved into the new Fleet Center in 1995–96.

Larry Bird and the Celtics beat the Houston Rockets in the 1986 NBA Finals.

tive title in 1962–63, but John Havlicek arrived the same season. Auerbach stepped down as coach after the eighth straight title in 1965–66. He handed the reins to Russell, who retired as player-coach following the second of back-to-back titles in 1968–69. (An important historical note is that when he was named to replace Auerbach, Russell became the first African American coach of any major professional sports team.)

Center Dave Cowens helped the team win a pair of titles in the 1970s, while the 1980s belonged to Larry Bird. A three-time league MVP, Bird teamed with Robert Parish and Kevin McHale to lead Boston to three more championships.

After winning their 16th title in 1985–86 and losing in the 1986–87 finals, the Celtics fell on hard times. The aging club was able to make the playoffs for several seasons after that but did not challenge for a title. Bird retired before the 1992–93 season, and Boston missed the playoffs the following year. In 1996–97, the

The Celtics helped integrate pro basketball in 1950, when they made Duquesne's Charles Cooper the first African American ever selected in the league draft.

The Celtics beat the Phoenix Suns in one of the greatest games in NBA history in the 1976 finals. With the series tied 2–2, Boston won the pivotal fifth game 128–126 in three overtimes.

Paul Pierce is one of the Celtics' contemporary stars.

Celtics' fortunes reached their **nadir,** when the club's 15–67 record was the worst in its history.

The next season, however, Rick Pitino was hired as coach and began rebuilding the club. Shooting guard Paul Pierce arrived as a heralded rookie from Kansas in 1998–99. By 2001–02, when he averaged a career-best 26.2 points per game, Pierce was one of the top players in the NBA. More important, the Celtics were back in the postseason after winning 49 games—their highest total in 10 years—under Jim O'Brien, who took over as coach midway through 2000–01.

Before the 2003–04 season, former guard Danny

Ainge, who played on two NBA championship teams for the Celtics in the 1980s, was brought in as executive director of basketball operations. With Pierce as the centerpiece, Ainge began molding a club that he felt could return Boston to its former status as one of the league's elite teams. He also hired Glenn "Doc" Rivers as coach in 2004–05, and Boston won 45 games in Rivers' first season. The Celtics held off Philadelphia by two games that season to win their first Atlantic Division championship since 1991–92.

Guard Paul Pierce scored the 10,000th point of his Celtics career on March 12, 2004, in a game against the Indiana Pacers. Pierce reached that plateau faster than any other player in Boston's celebrated history.

"Doc" Rivers (left) led Boston to the division title in his first season as coach in 2004–05.

The Nets' relatively brief history has been a roller-coaster ride of dizzying heights, stunning drops, and twists and turns. The franchise began play in the American Basketball Association (ABA) in 1967. That fledgling league wanted a team in New York, the nation's marquee city. Instead, it got a squad of journeymen and **semipros** who played in a converted **armory** in Teaneck, New Jersey, and went by the name the New Jersey Americans.

The next year, the club changed its name to the New York Nets and moved to Commack Arena on Long Island. Thus began a series of **nomadic** adventures that took the team to five different arenas before finally settling in New Jersey— and taking the name New Jersey Nets—in 1977.

The original Americans won 36 games, but by 1968, the team was the ABA's worst at 17–61. The Nets acquired their first star in 1970, when they signed flashy, high-scoring forward Rick Barry. One year later, the team was in the ABA Finals. Though they lost that series to the Indiana Pacers, they won fans and exposure in New York City.

Barry was gone the next year, and the club quickly fell among the league also-rans again. But the Nets replaced Barry's star power and scoring

The Americans tied the Kentucky Colonels for the final postseason spot in the ABA's inaugural season, forcing a one-game playoff at Commack Arena on Long Island. When the teams arrived, however, they found the court in unplayable condition, and Kentucky won by forfeit.

Julius Erving starred for the Nets in their ABA days.

ability before the 1973–74 season by acquiring Julius
"Dr. J." Erving. His dazzling array of skills produced a
league-best 27.4 points per game. The Nets waltzed to
the ABA title in his first year with the club. Two years
later, the Nets won the last ABA championship.

The Nets (along with several other ABA teams)
joined the NBA in 1976, but their fortunes plum-
meted again as quickly as they had risen. Erving was
traded to the 76ers before the season began, and the

The Americans
changed their name
to the Nets in 1968
to rhyme with two
of New York's other
teams, the Mets and
the Jets. It originally
was a whimsical
suggestion by a
local sportswriter.

Buck Williams' jersey was retired in a ceremony in 1999.

Nets finished a league-worst 22–60. Over the next quarter-century, the team had some good players—including Buck Williams, the team's all-time leading scorer and rebounder, and the popular Drazen Petrovic, who was tragically killed at age 28 in a car accident in 1993. Still, the Nets managed only seven winning seasons in that span and won only one playoff series (it came in the 1983–84 season).

Finally in 2001–02, the Nets had their best NBA season. Newly acquired point guard Jason Kidd and young forward Kenyon Martin led coach Byron Scott's team to a 52–30 record and the club's first Atlantic Division title. The Nets beat Indiana, Charlotte, and Boston in the playoffs before Los Angeles ended their run in the NBA Finals.

Undaunted by that defeat, New Jersey won 49 games in 2002–03 and again reached the NBA Finals. The Nets played well, but lost in six games to the San Antonio Spurs.

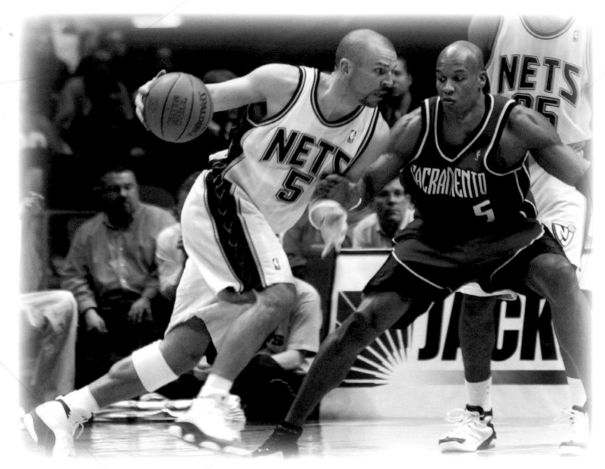

Jason Kidd has run the Nets' offense from his point guard position since joining the club in 2001–02.

With Kidd earning his third consecutive All-Star selection and Martin his first, the Nets won the Atlantic Division again the following season. But after an easy four-game sweep of the Knicks in the opening round, New Jersey's title hopes were dashed again, this time by eventual champion Detroit. The Pistons rallied from a three-games-to-two deficit to win an exciting seven-game series.

New Jersey's three-year run atop the Atlantic

Forward Kenyon Martin played a key role as the Nets made back-to-back trips to the NBA Finals.

Division abruptly ended in 2004–05, when Martin left the club after becoming a **free agent.** All-star swingman Vince Carter was acquired early in the season from Toronto and averaged 27.5 points per game for the Nets, but the club struggled, winning as many games as it lost. Still, a dramatic four-game winning streak to end the **regular season** lifted the Nets to a 42–40 record and into the playoffs.

In a memorable stretch of the 2003–04 season, the Nets won 10 consecutive games by 10 or more points. No NBA team had done that since the Washington Capitols nearly 60 years earlier.

Vince Carter was all smiles when he joined the Nets in December of 2004.

Point guard Jason Kidd became the first player in club history to lead the league in assists in consecutive years when he topped the NBA in both 2002–03 and 2003–04.

New Jersey was not able to sustain that success in the playoffs, and the Nets were swept away by the Miami Heat in the opening round. Still, four consecutive trips to the postseason (a first since the mid-1980s) left the Nets' roller coaster clearly back on the upswing again.

CHAPTER THREE

THE NEW YORK KNICKS

When the New York Knicks earned the first pick in the 1985 NBA draft, the club and its fans felt as if they'd won the lottery. Actually, the Knicks had won the lottery—the first NBA draft lottery. (Before 1985, only the poorest teams qualified for the top pick; now, every team that misses the playoffs has a chance. All these teams enter a drawing to determine the draft order.) And, as everyone knew, the first pick in the 1985 draft would be coveted center Patrick Ewing from Georgetown.

Former Knicks forward Bill Bradley was a Rhodes scholar who went on to become a United States senator.

The Knicks did indeed take Ewing in the draft, and his selection helped usher in the longest sustained streak of excellence in club history: 14 consecutive playoff appearances from 1988 to 2001, three division titles, and two Eastern Conference championships. And yet, the big prize—an NBA championship—eluded the Knicks during all those years.

That's an old story for New York. One of the most successful franchises since joining the Basketball Association of America in 1946, the Knicks often have come close but have managed to win only two titles.

In the early days of the franchise, the Knicks advanced to the NBA Finals three consecutive years, only to come up short each time.

New York's Nat "Sweetwater" Clifton was the first African American player to sign with an NBA team. The Knicks signed the former Harlem Globetrotters star in 1950.

They were led by Hall of Fame coach Joe Lapchick and All-Stars Carl Braun and Dick McGuire.

Then came a series of lean years until the arrival of center Willis Reed in 1964 and coach Red Holzman in 1967. New York's 1969–70 team roared to 60 regular-season victories and the Eastern Division title. That team featured guards Walt Frazier and Dick Barnett, forwards Dave DeBusschere and Bill Bradley, and Reed. After beating Baltimore and Milwaukee in the

Guard Walt Frazier was the top scorer on the Knicks' 1973 championship team.

Bill Bradley drove from the Knicks to the Hall of Fame and the U.S. Senate.

playoffs, the Knicks outlasted Los Angeles in seven games for their first NBA championship.

The final game that year provided one of the most dramatic moments in NBA history. Reed had suffered a torn thigh muscle in Game 5 and missed the next game. And without the Knicks' 6-foot-9, 235-pound center clogging the middle, the Lakers'

The Knicks won their first NBA title in 1970.

Wilt Chamberlain had his way in Game 6, scoring 45 points and hauling down 27 rebounds. Los Angeles breezed to a 135–113 rout that tied the series.

As the teams warmed up in Madison Square Garden for the finale, Reed stayed in the locker room for treatment. When he worked his way to the court shortly before tip-off, a steady roar built to a crescendo. The Lakers were stunned, and the Knicks were pumped at the sight of their star. Though clearly hobbled, Reed quickly made a pair of jumpers to open the scoring in the game. He would not score again, but he didn't have to. The Knicks rode the emotion of his appearance to an easy 113–99 triumph.

New York won 52, 48, and 57 games the next three seasons. The Knicks won the league title again by downing the Lakers in five games in the 1973 finals.

By the mid-1970s, the Knicks' run was over. They had several losing seasons before bottoming out with a last-place

> **Bernard King led the NBA by averaging 32.9 points per game in 1984–85. He is the only Knicks player ever to lead the league in scoring.**

Center Patrick Ewing helped make the Knicks a perennial playoff team.

finish in 1984–85. Then came the selection of Ewing. Though it took a few seasons, the club was back in the playoffs by 1987–88. Under coach Pat Riley from 1991–92 through 1994–95, New York posted 50 or more wins for four consecutive seasons and won two Atlantic Division titles. The 1994 team advanced to the finals before losing a seven-game heartbreaker to Houston. In 1999, the Knicks were the eighth and final seed in the East, but advanced all the way to the NBA Finals again. This time, they were **stymied** by San Antonio in five games.

Ewing's last season with the Knicks was in 2000, when New York earned its 13th consecutive playoff berth. Prolific scorer Latrell Sprewell helped New York run its streak to 14 in 2000–01 before the club fell short of the postseason in 2001–02 and 2002–03.

Though the Knicks returned to the playoffs in 2003–04, their stay in the postseason was brief— they were swept by the Nets in four games in the opening round.

The early exit brought wholesale changes the next year. Former star NBA guard Isiah Thomas was hired as president of basketball operations and revamped the club. The biggest change came after the 2004-05 season, when Thomas hired Hall of Famer Larry Brown to take over as coach. The Brooklyn native had guided the Pistons to consecutive appearances in the NBA Finals, including a championship in 2003-04.

In 1969–70, Knicks center Willis Reed became the first player to earn MVP honors for the All-Star Game, the regular season, and the NBA Finals in the same season.

Through the 2004–05 season, Knicks guard Stephon Marbury was one of only two players in NBA history with career averages of more than 20 points and eight assists per game. The other was Hall of Fame guard Oscar Robertson.

Some of the NBA's biggest stars have played for the 76ers franchise. They include Dolph Schayes in the club's early days, Wilt Chamberlain in the 1960s, Julius Erving in the 1970s and 1980s, and Allen Iverson since the 1990s. The wealth of individual talent has resulted in team success, too. Since joining the NBA in 1949–50, the club has won three league titles. Only the Celtics, Lakers, and Bulls have won more.

Actually, the club's first title came while the team played in Syracuse and was called the Nationals. Syracuse's roots went back to 1937. The club was one of six National Basketball League teams to survive the merger that resulted in the formation of the NBA in 1949.

At 6-foot-8, Schayes was one of the first big men who also had a **deft** shooting touch. With Schayes leading the way, the Nationals won 51 of 64 regular-season games. They advanced to the first NBA Finals before losing to Minneapolis. The Lakers foiled Syracuse's hopes again in 1954, but the Nationals won the 1955 title with a seven-game victory over Fort Wayne in the finals. In the last seconds of the decisive game, George King sank a free throw for a 92–91 lead and then stole the ball to preserve the victory.

Nationals owner Danny Biasone proposed a 24-second shot clock before the 1954–55 season. The clock revitalized the sport—and helped Syracuse overcome a 17-point deficit in the decisive game of the NBA Finals that season.

Dolph Schayes (No. 4) was one of the NBA's first all-around stars.

The club relocated to Philadelphia for the 1963–64 season and was renamed the 76ers.

Two years later, Philadelphia made big news by acquiring 7-foot-1 center Wilt Chamberlain from the San Francisco Warriors. Chamberlain was a Philadelphia native who had begun playing for the Warriors in 1959, when the club was located in his hometown. In 1961–62, he averaged an unbeliev-able 50.4 points and 25.7 rebounds a game for the Warriors. Against New York that season, he scored a

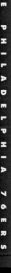

Wilt Chamberlain was a notoriously poor free-throw shooter who aver-aged only 51 per-cent for his career. But in his 100-point game while playing for the Warriors in 1962, he made 28 of his 32 free-throw tries.

Wilt Chamberlain (No. 13) was the most feared offensive player in NBA history.

record 100 points in a game. He is still the only player to reach that mark in an NBA game.

For all his prowess, the word on Chamberlain was that he couldn't win a championship. That changed in 1966–67. Teamed with fellow future Hall of Famers Hal Greer and Billy Cunningham, Chamberlain helped lead Philadelphia to a 68–13 record during the regular season. After ending Boston's eight-year run as NBA champions in the Eastern finals, the 76ers downed Chamberlain's old team, the Warriors, in six games to win the title.

Chamberlain played only one more year before being traded to Los Angeles, and the 76ers won just nine games in 1972–73. But the club didn't stay down long and soon acquired its next big superstar in 1976, when Julius Erving was purchased from the New York Nets. "Dr. J" made an immediate impact, playing every game his first season with Philadelphia and helping the team win 50 regular-season games and its first Atlantic Division championship.

The 76ers reached the NBA Finals that year, only to lose to the Portland Trail Blazers in six games. With Erving leading the way, Philadelphia

Hall of Famer Billy Cunningham played for the NBA champion 76ers in 1966–67 and coached the 1982–83 team that won the title.

Billy Cunningham (No. 32) played for and coached championship teams in Philadelphia.

won conference championships again in 1979–1980 and 1981–82, only to have powerful Los Angeles Lakers teams end their run at each title.

Finally in 1982–83, Philadelphia broke through. After roaring to a 65–17 record during the regular season, the 76ers were unstoppable in the playoffs. They won 12 of 13 postseason games, including a four-game sweep of the Lakers in the finals to win the league championship.

The 76ers have not won the title since then, but they have been a playoff team more often than not. That includes a stretch of five consecutive years in the postseason from 1998–99 through 2002–03,

Acrobatic "Dr. J" (Julius Erving) was a crowd pleaser and a Hall of Famer.

Allen Iverson won four NBA scoring titles in his first nine seasons in the league.

In Game 2 of the Eastern Conference semifinals against Toronto in 2001, Allen Iverson scored 54 points. In one stretch, he had 19 consecutive points for the 76ers, who won 97–92.

all under Hall of Fame coach Larry Brown (who went on to lead Detroit to the NBA title in 2003–04).

Allen Iverson is the club's latest star. He is a prolific scorer who was the NBA's MVP in 2000–01, when he averaged 31.1 points per game and led the 76ers to the finals, where they lost to the Lakers. In 2004–05, Iverson led the league in scoring for the fourth time in his nine-year career, averaging 30.7 points per game.

CHAPTER FIVE

THE TORONTO RAPTORS

Isiah Thomas and the Raptors burst onto the scene in 1995.

T he city of Toronto, Canada, waited almost 50 years for the
return of professional basketball. Since 1995, the fast-rising
Raptors have made its happy hoops fans wonder why they had to
wait so long.

The Raptors may be only a decade old, but basketball in
Toronto goes back to 1946. That's when the Toronto Huskies played

Besides the Raptors, other names considered for the Toronto expansion team were the Beavers, the Bobcats, the Dragons, and the Grizzlies.

their one and only season in the old Basketball Association of America. In 1993, the NBA announced that basketball would return to Toronto. It granted the city an expansion team, set to begin play in the 1995–96 season.

Toronto fans entered a contest to choose the team's name and colors. The winning name was

Marcus Camby was one of the Raptors' earliest stars.

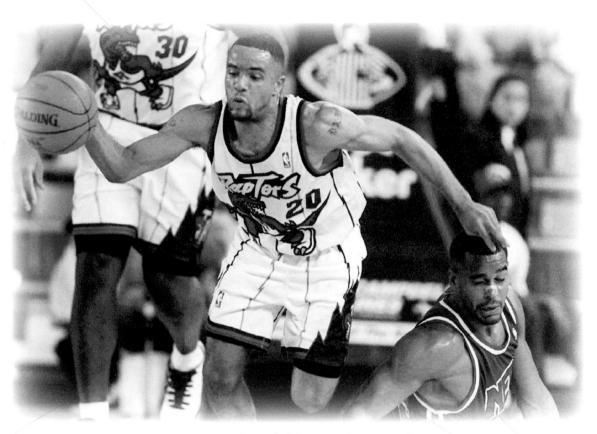

Damon Stoudamire led the expansion Raptors by averaging 19.1 points per game in 1995.

Raptors, after a dinosaur in the movie *Jurassic Park*. Isiah Thomas, the retired point guard from the Detroit Pistons, was put in charge of building the team roster. Canadian fans hungry for NBA basketball snapped up season tickets at a rapid rate.

Like any expansion team, the Raptors struggled at first, and they won a modest 21 games in their first season. Fans were patient, however, and they enjoyed watching young stars like Damon Stoudamire and Marcus Camby grow and improve. In 1999, another young Raptor, Vince Carter, won the Rookie of the Year award. The future looked bright.

The Raptors played their first two seasons in Toronto's SkyDome (now called the Rogers Centre) home to baseball's Blue Jays.

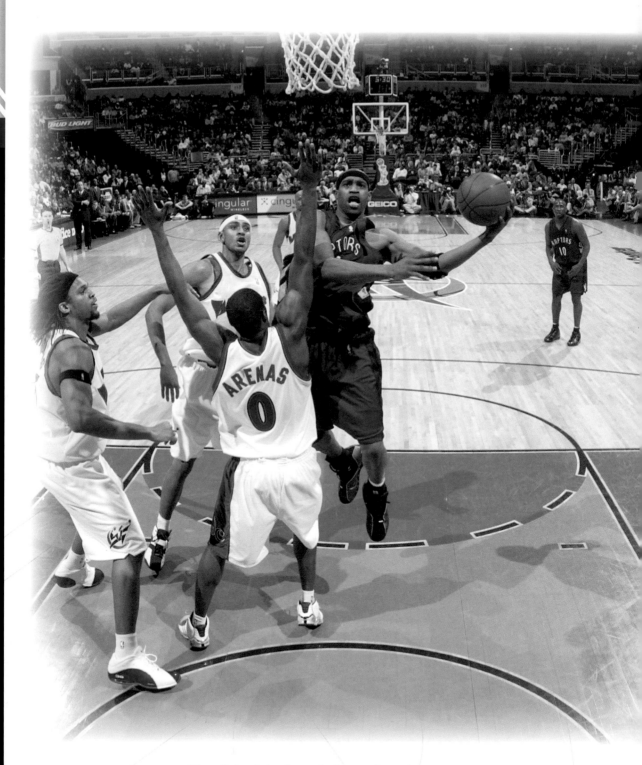

Vince Carter helped turn the Raptors into winners.

The 1999–2000 season held several firsts for Toronto. Carter, nicknamed "Air Canada," became the first Raptor to appear in an NBA All-Star Game. His high-flying dunks helped lead the team to its first winning season (a 45–37 regular-season record) and into the playoffs for the first time as well. The Raptors lost the first-ever postseason game played in Canada to the New York Knicks to close out an exciting series.

Toronto made the playoffs in each of the next two seasons. In 2000–01, under Hall of Fame coach Lenny Wilkens, the Raptors won 47 regular-season games (still the club record) and finished in second place in the NBA's Central Division (their highest finish ever). The club then won its first postseason series, beating the mighty New York Knicks three games to two in the opening round before falling to eventual conference-champion Philadelphia in seven games.

Carter was hailed as one of the NBA's rising stars, and the Raptors as one of the league's up-and-coming teams. But after a third consecutive playoff appearance in 2001–02, Toronto fell back

When Vince Carter was traded to the New Jersey Nets early in the 2004–05 season, he stood as the franchise's career leader in 10 different categories, including scoring and three-point field goals.

Jalen Rose averaged a team-best 18.5 points per game in 2004–05.

Players such as young forward Chris Bosh have Raptors' fans optimistic about the future.

on tough times, posting losing seasons the next two years. Carter asked to be traded the following season and was granted his wish early in 2004–05, going to the division-rival Nets in exchange for three players and a pair of first-round draft choices.

Though the Raptors went on to win only 33 games that year, they thrilled fans with one of the highest-scoring offenses in the league. Small forward Jalen Rose led the team by averaging 18.5 points per game, and young Chris Bosh gave the team an emerging star around whom to build.

All that—plus the high draft choices obtained in the Carter trade—means the future, like the past, looks bright for NBA action in Toronto.

Toronto increased its scoring average by 14.3 points per game in 2004–05 over 2003–04. That was the third-largest season-to-season improvement in NBA history.

TIME LINE

1946 The Boston Celtics and the New York Knicks begin play as charter members of the BAA (the forerunner to the NBA)

1949 The Syracuse Nationals make their NBA debut

1957 Boston wins its first NBA title

1959 The Celtics win the first of a record eight consecutive league championships

1963 The Nationals move from Syracuse to Philadelphia and become the 76ers

1967 The 76ers win the NBA title and stop Boston's string of eight consecutive championships

1967 The New Jersey Americans (now the Nets) begin play as charter members of the ABA

1970 The Knicks win their first NBA title

1974 The Nets win the first of two ABA titles in three seasons

1995 Toronto welcomes the Raptors

1999 The Raptors' Vince Carter is named Rookie of the Year

2003 New Jersey reaches its second consecutive NBA Finals

STAT STUFF

TEAM RECORDS

TEAM	ALL-TIME RECORD	NBA TITLES (MOST RECENT)	NUMBER OF TIMES IN PLAYOFFS	TOP COACH (WINS)
Boston	2,737–1,856	16 (1985–86)	45	Red Auerbach (795)
*New Jersey	1,366–1,724	2 (1975–76)	21	Kevin Loughery (297)
New York	2,343–2,246	2 (1972–73)	38	Red Holzman (613)
Philadelphia	2,388–2,030	3 (1982–83)	43	Billy Cunningham (454)
Toronto	314–474	0	3	Lenny Wilkens (113)

*includes ABA

NBA ATLANTIC CAREER LEADERS (THROUGH 2004–05)

TEAM	CATEGORY	NAME (YEARS WITH TEAM)	TOTAL
Boston	Points	John Havlicek (1962–1978)	26,395
	Rebounds	Bill Russell (1956–1969)	21,620
New Jersey	Points	Buck Williams (1981–89)	10,440
	Rebounds	Buck Williams (1981–89)	7,576
New York	Points	Patrick Ewing (1985–2000)	23,665
	Rebounds	Patrick Ewing (1985–2000)	10,759
Philadelphia	Points	Hal Greer (1958–1973)	21,586
	Rebounds	Dolph Schayes (1948–1964)	11,256
Toronto	Points	Vince Carter (1998–2004)	9,420
	Rebounds	Antonio Davis (1999–2003)	2,803

MORE STAT STUFF

MEMBERS OF THE NAISMITH MEMORIAL NATIONAL BASKETBALL HALL OF FAME

BOSTON

PLAYER	POSITION	DATE INDUCTED
Nate (Tiny) Archibald	Guard	1991
Red Auerbach	Coach	1968
Dave Bing	Forward	1990
Larry Bird	Forward	1998
Walter Brown	Owner	1965
Bob Cousy	Guard	1970
Dave Cowens	Center	1991
Wayne Embry	Contributor	1999
John Havlicek	Forward	1983
Tom Heinsohn	Forward	1986
Bob Houbregs	Forward	1987
Bailey Howell	Guard	1997
K. C. Jones	Guard	1989
Sam Jones	Guard	1983
Alvin (Doggie) Julian	Coach	1967
Clyde Lovellette	Forward	1988
Ed Macauley	Center	1960
Pete Maravich	Guard	1987
Bob McAdoo	Center	2000
Kevin McHale	Forward	1999
Bill Mokray	Contributor	1965
Robert Parish	Center	2003
Andy Phillip	Guard	1961
Frank Ramsey	Guard	1981
Arnie Risen	Center	1998
Bill Russell	Center	1974
John (Honey) Russell	Coach	1964
Bill Sharman	Guard	1975
John Thompson	Coach	1999
Bill Walton	Center	1993

NEW JERSEY

PLAYER	POSITION	DATE INDUCTED
Nate Archibald	Guard	1991
Rick Barry	Guard	1987
Larry Brown	Coach	2002
Lou Carnesecca	Coach	1992
Chuck Daly	Coach	1994
Julius Erving	Forward	1993
Bob McAdoo	Center	2000
Drazen Petrovic	Guard	2002
Willis Reed	Center	1981

NEW YORK

PLAYER	POSITION	DATE INDUCTED
Walt Bellamy	Forward	1993
Bill Bradley	Forward	1982
Dave DeBusschere	Forward	1982
Walt Frazier	Guard	1987
Harry Gallatin	Guard	1991
Tom Gola	Center	1975
Red Holzman	Coach	1986
Joe Lapchick	Forward	1966
Jerry Lucas	Forward	1979
Slater Martin	Guard	1981
Bob McAdoo	Center	2000
Al McGuire	Guard	1992
Dick McGuire	Guard	1993
Earl Monroe	Guard	1990
Willis Reed	Center	1981

MORE STAT STUFF

MEMBERS OF THE NAISMITH MEMORIAL NATIONAL BASKETBALL HALL OF FAME

PHILADELPHIA PLAYER	POSITION	DATE INDUCTED
Larry Brown	Coach	2002
Al Cervi	Guard	1984
Wilt Chamberlain	Center	1978
Billy Cunningham	Forward	1986
Julius Erving	Forward	1993
Hal Greer	Guard	1981
Alex Hannum	Forward	1998
Bailey Howell	Forward	1997
Earl Lloyd	Forward	2003
Moses Malone	Center	2001
Bob McAdoo	Center	2000
Jack Ramsay	Coach	1992
Dolph Schayes	Forward	1972
George Yardley	Forward	1996

TORONTO PLAYER	POSITION	DATE INDUCTED
Lenny Wilkens	Guard/Coach	1989

GLOSSARY

armory—a building for housing military equipment or personnel

deft—skillful

defunct—no longer active; closed down

flagship—the most notable of a particular group

free agent—an athlete who has finished his contract with one team and is eligible to sign with another

nadir—the lowest point

NBA Finals—a seven-game series between the winners of the NBA's Eastern and Western Conference championships

nomadic—wandering in search of a permanent place

playoffs—a four-level postseason elimination tournament involving eight teams from each conference; levels include two rounds of divisional playoffs, a conference championship round, and the NBA Finals (all series are best of seven)

regular season—describes an 82-game schedule in which each of the NBA's 30 teams plays 52 games within its conference, 16 of which are within its division; a team plays two games against each team outside its conference, one at home and one away

semipros—short for semiprofessionals; describes individuals who play a sport for money or some sort of gain, but who don't view playing the sport as their full-time occupation

sixth man—a basketball team's key substitute, the first player off the bench after the starting five

stymied—blocked

FOR MORE INFORMATION ABOUT THE ATLANTIC DIVISION AND THE NBA

BOOKS

Frisch, Aaron. *The History of the Toronto Raptors.* Mankato, Minn.: Creative Education, 2002.

Goodman, Michael E. *The History of the New Jersey Nets.* Mankato, Minn.: Creative Education, 2002.

Goodman, Michael E. *The History of the New York Knicks.* Mankato, Minn.: Creative Education, 2002.

Goodman, Michael E. *The History of the Philadelphia 76ers.* Mankato, Minn.: Creative Education, 2002.

Macnow, Glen. *Sports Great: Allen Iverson.* Berkeley Heights, N.J.: Enslow Publishers, 2003.

Mandell, Judith. *Super Sports Star Gary Payton.* Berkeley Heights, N.J.: Enslow Publishers, 2001.

Nichols, John. *The History of the Boston Celtics.* Mankato, Minn.: Creative Education, 2002.

Plum-Ucci, Carol. *Super Sports Star Stephon Marbury.* Berkeley Heights, N.J.: Enslow Publishers, 2002.

Rappoport, Ken. *Jason Kidd: Leader on the Court.* Berkeley Heights, N.J.: Enslow Publishers, 2004.

Torres, John Albert. *Vince Carter: Slam Dunk Artist.* Berkeley Heights, N.J.: Enslow Publishers, 2004.

ON THE WEB

Visit our home page for lots of links
about the Atlantic Division teams:
http://www.childsworld.com/links

Note to Parents, Teachers, and Librarians: We routinely verify our Web links to make sure they are safe, active sites—so encourage your readers to check them out!

INDEX

ABOUT THE AUTHORS

Jim Gigliotti is a former editor at the National Football League who now is a freelance writer based in Southern California. His writing credits include *Baseball: A Celebration* (with James Buckley Jr.) and *Stadium Stories: USC Trojans,* as well as a dozen children's and young adult books on various sports and personalities.

Robert E. Schnakenberg has written eight books on sports for young readers, including *Teammates: John Stockton and Karl Malone* and *Scottie Pippen: Reluctant Superstar.* He lives in Brooklyn, New York.